Surviving sinking ships

During times of war, ships are often wrecked by enemy bombs. The crew are forced to jump overboard in order to survive and are left stranded in the middle of the ocean. Many sailors over the years have found themselves alone at sea, forced to survive by whatever means they had. One sailor who survived against all the odds was Poon Lim, who was alone, drifting on a tiny raft for over 100 days in the Atlantic Ocean.

These men survived an attack on their submarine during World War II and are clinging to their life rafts, in the middle of the sea, waiting to be rescued.

Thrill seekers

While some have no choice about surviving at sea, others choose to test themselves against the mighty oceans. Norwegian explorer, Thor Heyerdahl, and modern adventurer, Ellen MacArthur, have both tested their skills and strengths while at sea. Today boats have amazing technology for sailors to use and are much faster and stronger than early ships, yet the survival skills of these two adventurers were pushed to the limit as they endured pain, loneliness and fear.

MUTINY AT SEA

William Bligh (1754–1817) became famous for being involved in one of the most notorious mutinies at sea. Forced into a rowing boat with just a handful of loyal crew, Bligh was cast adrift with little food or water. He had to reach land without the help of a map or compass or he and his crew would die at sea.

Aboard the HMS *Bounty*

In 1787, Lieutenant William Bligh took command of a ship called the *Bounty*. His task was to sail to Tahiti to find **breadfruit trees**. It was hoped that the trees could be grown in the Caribbean to feed the slaves there. The voyage to Tahiti was difficult. The crew tried for a month to sail around Cape Horn, but the stormy weather forced them to take the long route around the Cape of Good Hope. Food and rations on board ran low because of the delay and the crew became tense and angry.

*On board the Bounty Bligh kept a **ship's log**, which showed that he was reluctant to give out harsh punishments. But many of the crew feared his anger and bad temper.*

Breadfruit grow on trees that can produce anywhere between 50 and 200 fruits in a year. It is said that when the fruit is roasted, it tastes like freshly baked bread.

DIFFICULT & DANGEROUS

Survival at Sea

SIMON LEWIS

W

FRANKLIN WATTS

LONDON•SYDNEY

An Appleseed Editions book

First published in 2008 by Franklin Watts

Paperback edition 2009

Franklin Watts
338 Euston Road, London NW1 3BH

Franklin Watts Australia
Hachette Children's Books
Level 17/207 Kent St, Sydney, NSW 2000

© 2008 Appleseed Editions

Appleseed Editions Ltd
Well House, Friars Hill, Guestling, East Sussex TN35 4ET

Created by Q2AMedia
Series Editor: Jean Coppendale; Book Editor: Corrine Ochiltree
Senior Art Designers: Ashita Murgai, Nishant Mudgal
Designer: Shilpi Sarkar; Picture Researcher: Lalit Dalal
Line Artists: Amit Tayal, Sibi N.D
Illustrators: Aadil Ahmed Siddiqui, Mahender Kumar, Sanyogita Lal

ISBN 978 0 7496 9281 0

Dewey classification: 910.4' 5

All words in **bold** can be found in the glossary on page 30.

Website information is correct at time of going to press. However, the publishers cannot accept liability for any information or links found on third-party websites.

A CIP catalogue for this book is available from the British Library.

Picture credits
t=top b=bottom c=centre l=left r=right m=middle
Cover: Q2AMedia
Marc Stewart: 4, Getty Images: 5t, Gerard Cazade/ Corbis: 5b, Bettmann/ Corbis: 6t, Scott Leigh: 6b, Dennis Bone: 7, Robert Crook: 11, Bettmann/ Corbis: 12, Getty Images: 13, Leo/ Shutterstock: 15t, The Kon-Tiki Museum/ www.kon-tiki.no/ : 16, 17, 18, 20t, Kenneth William Caleno/ Shutterstock: 20b, Jeremy Smith/ Shutterstock: 25b, Corbis: 26 AFP: 27, 28, Claes Torstensson: 29l Getty Images: 29r

Printed in China

Franklin Watts is a division of Hachette Children's Books, an Hachette UK company.
www.hachette.co.uk

Contents

SURVIVAL AT SEA

The thought of being lost at sea is terrifying. But there are tales of people who have been alone in vast oceans, without food or water, and have survived. They tell of being surrounded by sharks, scorched by the sun or frozen by icy waters. Their stories are both horrifying and fascinating. Yet over the centuries people have also seen the sea as a challenge to test their survival skills, endurance and strength.

Ocean explorers

Throughout history explorers have taken to the seas and travelled vast distances to discover new countries around the world. Although exploring can seem exciting and adventurous, events can often go quickly and sometimes tragically wrong at sea. Captain William Bligh and some of the crew of the *Bounty* discovered this to their cost. Cast adrift at sea, they managed to survive their difficult and dangerous ordeal.

Captain Bligh and his crew sailed the magnificent ship, the Bounty, *to Tahiti where the famous mutiny took place.*

Destination Tahiti

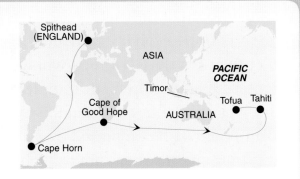

This map shows the route the Bounty *took from England to Tahiti. The journey to Tahiti was very long – it took almost a year.*

The Bounty *was a **cutter** ship. It only had 45 men on board and so did not have any special security officers.*

Tahiti at last

At last the *Bounty* reached Tahiti. This green and beautiful island was like paradise to the sailors. The sea was calm and inviting, the weather warm and sunny, and the Tahitian people were gentle, fun-loving and welcoming. Bligh's crew lived on the island for five months before the breadfruit trees were ready to be transported and the winds were right for the ship to set sail again.

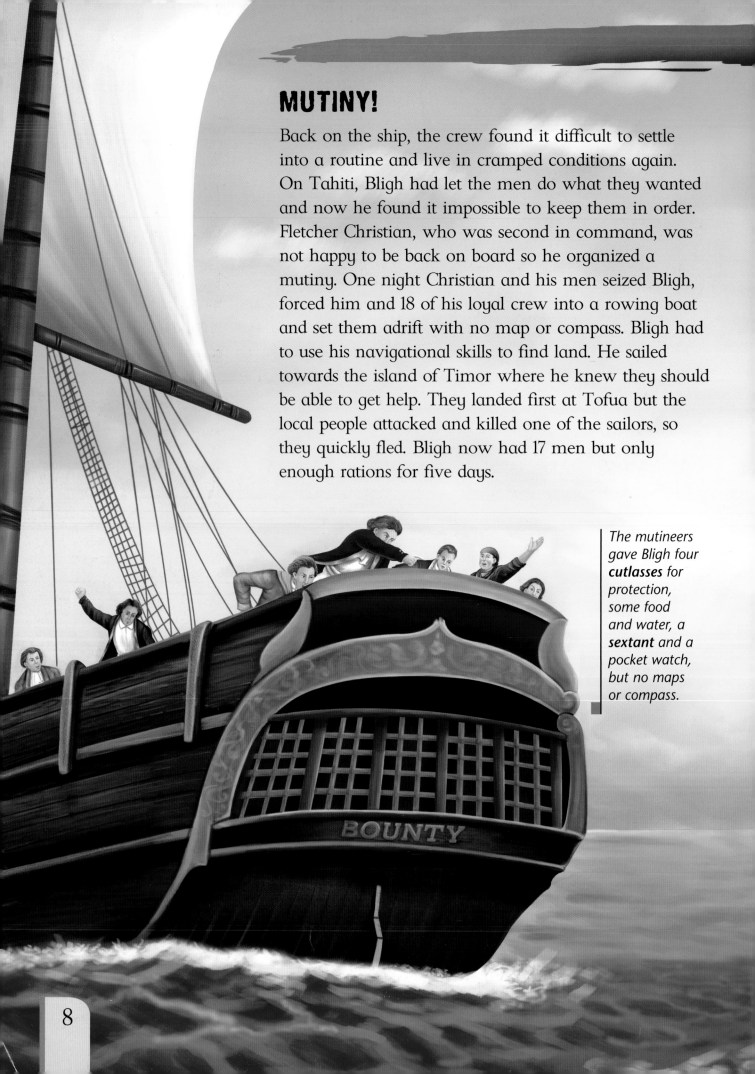

MUTINY!

Back on the ship, the crew found it difficult to settle into a routine and live in cramped conditions again. On Tahiti, Bligh had let the men do what they wanted and now he found it impossible to keep them in order. Fletcher Christian, who was second in command, was not happy to be back on board so he organized a mutiny. One night Christian and his men seized Bligh, forced him and 18 of his loyal crew into a rowing boat and set them adrift with no map or compass. Bligh had to use his navigational skills to find land. He sailed towards the island of Timor where he knew they should be able to get help. They landed first at Tofua but the local people attacked and killed one of the sailors, so they quickly fled. Bligh now had 17 men but only enough rations for five days.

*The mutineers gave Bligh four **cutlasses** for protection, some food and water, a **sextant** and a pocket watch, but no maps or compass.*

> *'Just before sunrise Mr Christian…
> and several officers came into my
> cabin while I was fast asleep, and
> seizing me tied my hands with a
> cord and threatened instant death
> if I made the least noise.
> Mr Christian had a cutlass and
> the others armed with musquets
> and bayonets. I was now carried
> on deck in my shirt, in torture
> with a severe bandage round my
> wrists behind my back.'*
>
> From William Bligh's log.

Drinking blood

While Christian and the **mutineers** sailed back to Tahiti on the *Bounty*, Bligh and his crew were left starving at sea. Fierce storms raged and the men were cold, wet and exhausted from constantly **bailing** water from the boat. They caught and ate sea birds, giving the blood to the weakest men to drink. After four weeks, they landed at Restoration Island off the coast of Australia where they found food and drinking water. But they had to row on and after 48 days they finally reached the island of Timor.

Bligh's route to safety

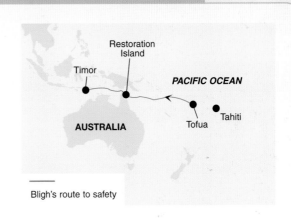

Bligh's route to safety

Bligh and his loyal crew landed safely on Timor near Java in the Pacific Ocean on 12 June 1789. They had travelled an incredible distance of 670 km.

The aftermath

Bligh and his men were safe at last, but now Bligh wanted to catch and punish the mutineers. A ship was sent to find them. Some were found on the island of Tahiti and brought back to England, where they were **tried** and hanged. Fletcher Christian escaped to the Pitcairn Islands with some of the other mutineers and a group of Tahitian men and women. They started a **colony** that still exists today. Christian was never caught but died in a fight between the Tahitians and mutineers. William Bligh went on to hold many more positions within the British Navy and served under Admiral Nelson in 1801.

*After the mutiny several mutineers, led by Fletcher Christian, and some men and women from Tahiti, decided to settle in the beautiful Pitcairn Islands in the Pacific Ocean. Their **descendants** still live there.*

What makes a good leader?

Some historians have written about Captain Bligh's cruelty. They say that he was a bad leader and that he had his crew whipped and punished for little reason. Others believe Bligh was fair and looked after his men well. What do you think makes a good leader? You could find out more about Captain Bligh. What good and bad qualities did he have? Note them down in two columns, headed GOOD and BAD, and weigh up the evidence for yourself.

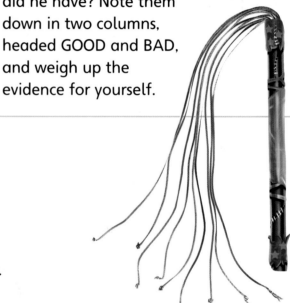

HORRORS OF WAR

During World War II many ships were attacked by submarines, and their crews killed or left to drown in shark-infested seas. When the SS Fort Buckingham was hit, a few sailors managed to escape the wreckage and scramble aboard lifeboats, but their ordeal was only just beginning...

Sinking ship!

Just before midnight on 9 January 1944, the German submarine *U.188* fired two **torpedoes** at the SS *Fort Buckingham*, a British merchant ship. The boat sank in about five minutes. Only 51 of the 89 sailors on board survived. These men jumped into the sea and clambered on to five lifeboats. No distress signal had been sent out from the ship and it was not due in port for another two weeks.

'We huddled together as best we could and as the night got colder we shared out our few clothes in order to make the best of our first night adrift.'
An account by Norman Gibson, an apprentice seaman on board the *Fort Buckingham*.

The **Kriegsmarine**, the German Navy, used submarines to attack **Allied** ships carrying food and equipment to support their forces in war zones.

Torpedoes were used to damage and destroy ships. They were fired from submarines and launched from battleships.

Cold and hungry

Many of the men were wearing very few clothes or none at all. At night they slept close together for warmth and dozed in the daytime. There was little food or water. After 11 days at sea, two of the lifeboats were spotted by a passing ship that sent a message saying help was needed to find the others. Three aircraft left Ceylon (now Sri Lanka) to search the area but one crashed into the sea on take-off and the crew was killed. Eventually, the remaining lifeboats were found and rescued. Only 46 men survived.

Blasted apart

The *U.188* continued prowling the Arabian Sea. On 22 January 1944, Captain Luedden, who was in charge of the submarine, sighted the SS *Fort La Maune*, which had left the port of Bari, Italy, and was heading for Bombay. At 8pm two watch-keepers on board the ship thought they saw **porpoises** - then, to their horror they realized it was a torpedo heading straight for them. The torpedo tore open the **port side** and the ship started to sink. The 50 sailors on board rushed to reach the two motorized lifeboats.

The U.188 had orders to sink all Allied merchant ships in the Arabian Sea and to take any valuable cargo it could capture back to Germany.

Extreme weather

The survivors decided to head for Socotra, an island off the coast of Somalia, East Africa. The journey would take 10 to 15 days and food and water were strictly rationed. At night, the sailors tied the lifeboats together so they would not drift apart. During the day the men were burned by the scorching sun, and by night they froze as the temperatures **plummeted**. Lack of water soon became a serious problem for them.

An Allied merchant ship sinks after a torpedo attack. Once a ship was hit it would sink very quickly and the chances of the crew surviving were small.

Squeezing fish

One of the men on board the lifeboat had heard that if fish were cut into cubes and then squeezed, they would give fresh water. He made a hook and caught several fish but failed to get any water. Then he boiled sea water and collected the **condensation** from the steam in a can. Although he managed to produce some drinking water, there was barely enough for one man! Meanwhile, unknown to the survivors, they were being carried further away from the search area.

Daggers and rifles

Nearly two weeks later, the sailors sighted land - Mukalla, on the coast of Arabia. As they neared the shore, they heard the drone of aeroplane engines overhead and fired two smoke **flares** into the sky. The planes saw the lifeboats, but could not land because locals armed with daggers and rifles had gathered on the beach and would not let the survivors come ashore. The pilots dropped the survivors a container of fresh water and a note saying 'Help is coming'. Two days later the survivors were rescued at last.

Exhausted survivors of the Fort La Maune *excitedly fired flares in the hope that the rescue planes would spot them.*

14

Could YOU survive?

Today, lifeboats must contain certain equipment, which includes:

- a knife
- 2 sponges
- 3 tin openers
- a pair of scissors
- a first aid kit
- a whistle
- 4 rocket flares
- 6 hand flares
- a daylight signalling mirror plus instructions
- fishing tackle
- fresh water
- 1 drinking vessel
- anti-seasickness medicine

If you were lost at sea for six weeks, how would you use this equipment to survive?

VOYAGE INTO THE PAST

In 1947, Norwegian explorer Thor Heyerdahl (1914–2002) began a dangerous journey that no one thought he would ever survive. He built a raft, called the **Kon-Tiki**, that was a copy of a 13th-century raft, and he set sail from South America towards Polynesia. Experts believed that he and his crew were sailing to certain death.

Heyerdahl's journey

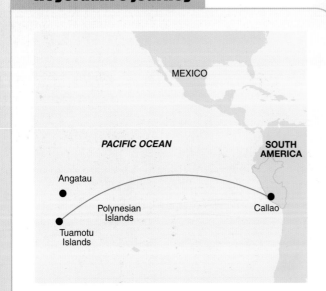

The route taken by the Kon-Tiki was one Thor Heyerdahl thought early South Americans may have used to reach Tahiti.

Heyerdahl checking the mast of the Kon-Tiki. The raft was towed out of the harbour at Callao in Peru. Once at sea, the raft and its crew were on their own.

Doomed journey

Experts believed that the *Kon-Tiki* was too small and flimsy for the open seas and that the crew would be washed overboard. They also thought the raft would be continually drenched by sea water, which would ruin all the supplies on board. They warned that the ropes holding the logs together would wear away within weeks, causing the raft to collapse. However, Heyerdahl was convinced that his raft would withstand the voyage. He and his crew of five men set sail on 27 April 1947 and their amazing adventure began.

Alone at sea

Strong winds helped to push the *Kon-Tiki* along but no one knew how to steer the raft. The seas were so rough that it took two of them to try and keep the raft on course, using the heavy oar, while the others slept as best they could. By the third day, Heyerdahl noticed that the balsawood logs were slowly soaking up water. This turned out to be a good thing, because the ropes binding them together were slowly pressing into the wood rather than rubbing against it, stopping them from being cut as the experts had predicted.

The Kon-Tiki *was built from balsa logs and bound together with* **hemp** *ropes. No nails or other metals were used. The sail was made of canvas, the cabin of bamboo with banana leaves for the roof and the steering oar was made of mangrove wood.*

Flying fish

After about a week, the sea grew calmer and the days on board began to fall into a routine. Food was not a problem - there were shoals of mackerel and swordfish, as well as squid and huge blue sharks. At night, flying fish leapt over the raft - many fell on board and were cooked and eaten the next day. One crewman even woke to find a sardine on his pillow. After about two months their fresh water ran out. The crew decided to press the juices out of fresh fish by twisting them in a piece of cloth.

During the voyage Thor Heyerdahl caught a large blue shark, which they cooked and ate on board.

Broken equipment

Heyerdahl and his crew took some modern equipment with them, including a radio transmitter, but on the first day it was drenched by sea water and stopped working. They also had a problem finding a long enough radio aerial. They attached a standard length aerial to a kite but the wind drove it into the sea. They tried attaching it to a balloon, but the blazing sun burnt holes in it. Then, unexpectedly, one night the radio burst into life - they had picked up a signal from someone in Los Angeles who was trying to contact a person in Sweden!

In torrential rain and high winds the crew battled desperately to keep the Kon-Tiki on course and to stop it from hitting any hidden reefs.

'A sea rose straight up under us, and we felt the Kon-Tiki being lifted up in the air. The great moment had come; we were riding on the wave back at breathless speed, our ramshackle raft creaking and groaning as she quivered under us. The excitement made one's blood boil'

Thor Heyerdahl, from his book, *The Kon-Tiki Expedition* (1950).

Deadly reef

On 30 July, the crew saw land for the first time since April, the island of Angatau in Polynesia. A jagged coral reef surrounded the island making it almost impossible to land, but the crew was sure that with the help of the islanders they could reach the shore safely. They were wrong. Strong winds pushed them back out to sea. They drifted for three days, finally heading for another island, which was also surrounded by a deadly reef. In heavy rain, strong winds and poor **visibility**, Thor Heyerdahl realized they would hit the reef and there was nothing they could do about it. They prepared to be hurled against the reef and for the *Kon-Tiki* to be smashed to pieces.

The Kon-Tiki has been rebuilt and is now on display at the Kon-Tiki Museum in Norway.

End of the Kon-Tiki

The crew held on as the raft was lifted up by the waves and smashed against the coral. The cabin splintered and the mast collapsed. Exhausted, battered and bruised, all the crew survived, but they had lost their raft. Carefully making their way over the sharp coral they **salvaged** the radio, cooking stove and other possessions that had been thrown across the reef. Then they waded to the **uninhabited** island. The next morning, they set up their radio and desperately tried to contact someone to say where they were and that they were safe. Eventually, someone answered and after several weeks on the tiny island, Thor Heyerdahl and his crew were rescued.

How would YOU survive?

Each member of the *Kon-Tiki* crew was allowed to take a couple of personal belongings with them for the journey, such as a guitar, paper and pencils and books. Write a list of things that you think would be useful to bring on a journey like this. Which items could you not live without? Why do you think these items are so important?

ALONE AT SEA

During World War II, Poon Lim (1917–91) was working on the British merchant ship the Ben Lomond as a second steward. On 23 November 1942, the ship was sailing in the Atlantic Ocean when it was attacked by a Nazi U-boat and hit by a torpedo. Poon Lim tied on a life jacket and jumped overboard. He was about to begin a terrible ordeal that would test his physical and mental strength to breaking point.

Poon Lim was born in China on Hainan Island.

Search for a raft

Along with the other survivors, Poon Lim swam away from the *Ben Lomond* as quickly as he could. Suddenly, there was a loud explosion on board as the boilers blew up and the ship disappeared beneath the waves. Poon Lim paddled in the water for two hours desperately searching for a life raft. He saw some lifeboats with other crew members in them but they were soon out of sight. Eventually, Poon Lim found an empty life raft and clambered on to it. Scared and exhausted, Poon Lim had to remain calm and decide what to do next.

The *Ben Lomond's* route

DUTCH GUIANA
AFRICA
BRAZIL
SOUTH AMERICA
ATLANTIC OCEAN
Cape Town

—— route of the Ben Lomond

The Ben Lomond was on its way from Cape Town in South Africa to Dutch Guiana (now Surinam) in northern South America.

Out of sight

To survive, Poon Lim had to ration the food and drink he found on the raft. He allowed himself a few mouthfuls of water and two biscuits twice a day. At first, he counted the days by tying knots in a rope, but later decided to count full moons. He swam around the raft every day to keep fit - always keeping an eye out for sharks.

Rescue at last?

Twice Poon Lim thought he was going to be rescued, once when a ship sailed close by but did not see him and once when a US Navy patrol plane passed by. They spotted him and dropped a marker buoy in the water, but a fierce storm blew the marker off course.

Learning to fish

These were the worst times for Poon Lim. He realized he could not expect to be rescued and that he must keep himself alive. Knowing that his food and water would soon run out, Poon Lim tore his life jacket apart and used the canvas to catch rainwater to drink. He made a fish hook from a spring in his torch, using a water jug as a hammer to bend it into shape. He attached the hook to some rope and made a fishing line, then used a bit of biscuit as bait and managed to catch fish, which he ate raw.

Poon Lim's home at sea

Poon Lim's wooden life raft was very small – only about 2.5 m square. It had four vertical poles at each corner, which held up the canopy. This provided Poon Lim with vital shade from the blazing sun. There was very little equipment on board the raft to help him survive. There were some tins of biscuits, a large water jug, some signal flares and a torch. These items, together with his own sheer determination, were all that Poon Lim had to keep him alive during his gruelling 133 days lost at sea.

One of the few items that Poon Lim found on board his raft, the water jug, came in very handy in his fight for survival.

Bird food

When there was no rain, Poon Lim had nothing to drink, so he decided to catch birds. For bait he used some of the fish he had caught, which he dried in the sun. He made a 'nest' out of seaweed and placed the rotting fish next to it to attract gulls. Eventually, a gull flew down to eat the fish and Poon Lim grabbed it. The gull fought back, stabbing him with its sharp beak and scratching him before he managed to kill it. He was so hungry and thirsty that he cut the bird up, chewed its raw flesh and drank its blood.

Poon Lim was incredibly clever and **inventive** in his efforts to find food and water while stranded at sea.

Signs of land

After 131 days at sea, Poon Lim noticed that the sea was a lighter green colour and there were more birds flying overhead. These were signs that he could be close to land. On the morning of the 133rd day, he saw a small fishing boat in the far distance. Jumping up and down and waving his arms about, Poon Lim shouted for help. The boat turned around and started heading towards him. The fishermen took him on board and told him he was at the mouth of the River Amazon in Brazil. Incredibly, he had crossed the Atlantic Ocean.

Before he was rescued, Poon Lim saw many ships in the distance. Although he waved and shouted, they were too far away and disappeared, leaving Poon Lim feeling helpless and depressed.

A great survivor

Poon Lim spent four weeks in a hospital in Brazil, building up his strength. He became a hero and the British Navy used many of his survival techniques in a **manual**, which was put in all of their life rafts. King George VI awarded Poon Lim the British Empire Medal and the USA granted him special permission to live permanently in the United States. Poon Lim later discovered that tragically only 11 of the *Ben Lomond*'s crew of 55 had survived.

*Poon Lim was awarded the British Empire Medal because of his **meritorious** service to the British Navy and his amazing bravery.*

'I hope no one will ever have to break it.'

Poon Lim said these words when told he held the record as the world's longest sea survivor.

Design a survival manual

Find out more about how Poon Lim survived his time at sea, how he made tools to catch fish and the techniques he used to catch birds for food. Write a short survival manual with simple drawings and giving instructions on how to survive at sea, based on Poon Lim's experiences.

RECORD BREAKER!

Ellen MacArthur (b. 1976) grew up far away from the sea, but she has broken some of the toughest sailing records there are. In 2005, she began her greatest challenge – to be the fastest person to sail solo around the world. This amazingly difficult race would test her physical and mental strength as well as her skills as a sailor.

At the start line

The race around the world began at Ushant, a small island off the north-west coast of France. Ellen MacArthur set sail in the *B&Q/Castorama* at 8.10am on 28 November 2004. During her first day, she battled against high winds and rough seas. She hardly slept at all on the first night because she felt 'sick with nerves'. Once the voyage was under way, Ellen only slept for about 15 minutes at a time. She survived on freeze-dried meals, which were mixed with water, and drank **desalinated** water. For a toilet, she had to use a bucket.

Ellen MacArthur's love of the sea and boats has led her to take part in lots of races and to break many sailing records.

'I became completely besotted with sailing and began to save every penny I could for a boat. Everything went into a money box which sat on my bedroom radiator for ten years.'

From her autobiography 'Ellen MacArthur - Taking on the World' (2002).

Battered and bruised

The *B&Q/Castorama* was a powerful craft and was built to sail through some of the worst weather conditions there are. The **winches** that operated the sail ropes were heavy to handle and caused MacArthur to strain every muscle in her body. Climbing the mast to repair sails was very dangerous in stormy weather. The climb could take nearly two hours and her legs were battered and covered in black and blue bruises.

— outward bound route
— homeward bound route

EUROPE
NORTH AMERICA
Falmouth
Finish　**Start**
Ushant
ASIA
AFRICA
ATLANTIC OCEAN
SOUTH AMERICA
AUSTRALIA
Cape of Good Hope
Cape Leeuwin
Cape Horn
SOUTHERN OCEAN
ANTARCTICA

On her solo journey around the world Ellen had to battle through some of the most dangerous seas around the Cape of Good Hope.

Ellen's boat was called B&Q/Castorama. *It was named after companies that sponsored her. The 23 m* **trimaran** *was built in Australia especially for Ellen who is only 1.57 m tall.*

Keeping ahead

As well as carrying out constant repairs and keeping the boat out of danger, Ellen had to keep her eye on how long she was taking on her voyage. She was aware that she had to beat the record set by the Frenchman, Francis Joyon of 72 days, 22 hours, 54 minutes, 22 seconds. One of the worst parts of the journey was rounding Cape Horn and battling the fierce storms and huge icebergs in the Southern Ocean. Then, beating the strong winds of the Southern Ocean, MacArthur entered the Atlantic, which was so calm that she lost five days lead-time.

End of the journey

Ellen was exhausted, both physically and mentally. She had nearly collided with a whale, badly burnt her arm on a generator and had to face terrible loneliness especially at Christmas time, when she missed her family and friends. But on the 7 February 2005, she crossed the finishing line beating the record set by Joyon. She had travelled 44,000 km in 71 days, 14 hours, 18 minutes, 33 seconds.

Ellen MacArthur on board the B&Q/Castorama *off the coast of Lorient, near Brittany in France, on 20 October 2004.*

Ellen MacArthur claimed she was, 'Exhausted but I'm elated to be here!' when she finally completed her round-the-world solo voyage.

'When I crossed the [finishing] line I felt like collapsing on the floor and just falling asleep. I was absolutely over the moon.'

From her autobiography
'Ellen MacArthur -
Taking on the World' (2002).

Could YOU cope?

Imagine that you are on a boat sailing around the world alone for over 70 days. What do you think would be the worst parts of the journey? What might be the best bits?

Glossary

Allies countries or nations joined together by a special treaty or agreement

bailing throwing water over the side of a boat to stop it from sinking

breadfruit trees these are found growing on Pacific islands and the fruit has the texture of bread

canopy a covering, usually made of cloth that is hung up to act as a roof for protection against the weather

colony a group of people who leave their native country to build a new home in another country

condensation the process by which vapour turns into a liquid

cutlass a short, curved sword that was once used by sailors as a weapon

cutter a small ship that is powered by sails or by oars

desalinate to remove salt from water so that it is safe to drink

descendants people whose roots can be traced back to a particular individual or group

flares lights, a bit like fireworks, that are sent high into the sky to signal that help is needed

hemp a tall plant that is native to Asia. Its tough fibre is used to make rope

inventive being resourceful and able to think creatively to solve problems

Kriegsmarine the German Navy, operating between 1935 and 1945

manual a small book that gives instructions to the reader

meritorious if a person or action deserves praise, they are said to be meritorious

mutineers people who take part in a mutiny

mutiny a rebellion or revolt against a person in charge

navigational skills these are needed in order to work out the position of ships while at sea. Reading the stars for direction and measuring the ship's speed are just two of these skills

plummet to drop down quickly or plunge

porpoises similar to a dolphin but with a blunt, rounded snout

port side the left side of a ship from the point of view of someone facing the front

rations a fixed amount of food or drink that is allowed to be consumed at one time

salvage to save items from danger or damage.

sextant an instrument used at sea to chart the position of a ship by measuring the distance in angles of the sun, moon and stars

ship's log a diary kept by the captain of a ship to record distance travelled, speed and other events that happen while at sea

torpedoes missiles that travel at high speed under water to blow up ships or submarines

tried people are tried in court when they are thought to have committed a crime

trimaran a boat with three hulls

uninhabited where no one lives or works

visibility the distance you can see clearly, which depends on the weather and other factors

winch a machine used to hoist or haul something up, such as a sail. A rope or chain is wound around a drum to move the item

Index

Webfinder

Captain William Bligh
http://www.lareau.org/bligh.html

Logbook of HMS *Bounty*
http://image.sl.nsw.gov.au/Ebind/safe1_47/a286/a286000.html

***U.188* attack**
http://scotland.users.ftech.net/u188p1.htm

Poon Lim
http://judkins.customer.netspace.net.au/survival.htm

Kon-Tiki
http://www.kon-tiki.no/Expeditions/demo/index.html

Ellen MacArthur
http://www.ellenmacarthur.com/